DESERT LIFE

Published for the American Museum of Natural History
The Natural History Press
Garden City, New York

Ruth Kirk

DESERT LIFE

With photographs by
Ruth and Louis Kirk

The Natural History Press, publisher for The American Museum of Natural History, is a division of Doubleday & Company, Inc. The Press is directed by an editorial board made up of members of the staff of both the Museum and Doubleday. The Natural History Press has its editorial offices at The American Museum of Natural History, Central Park West at Seventy-ninth Street, New York, New York 10024, and its business offices at 501 Franklin Avenue, Garden City, New York 11530.

DESIGNED BY EARL TIDWELL

DESERT LIFE

Desert is sand that blows in your hair and face,
and empty salt flats and dry mud hills
where the sun makes you sweat.

Desert also is sparse forests of cacti
and thorn bushes.

The desert also has springs with shade trees,
and water birds,
and fish left over from thousands of years ago
when this was grassland instead of desert.

In the desert, watch for birds with nests in cactus,
where thorns protect eggs and young,
and for road runners,
which hunt for insects
and lizards and baby mice.
About three hundred kinds of birds live in the
American Desert.

Watch for pack rats.

They build nests of sticks and stones
and bits of cactus.

They take your rings or money,
if they can find them.

Pack rats take anything shiny, if they can carry it.

Watch for peccaries,
the wild pigs of the desert,
which feed on cactus . . .

and for ringtail cats,
small cousins of bears,
which hunt for rodents . . .

and for coati mundis,
which eat plants and animals and birds and insects.
The coatis are Mexican animals,
but they now are moving north too.

A few desert animals are poisonous,
but most are not.
Even those that are poisonous,
such as rattlesnakes . . .

and gila monsters
don't often bite.
They usually try to get away from you.

Desert stretches across the southwest corner
of the United States and northwest Mexico.
The land is hot. Desert skies are blue and clear.
No clouds screen the sun's rays.
Few plants shade the soil and cool it.
The temperature of the air may be 120°F., or more,
on summer afternoons.
The temperature at the surface of the ground may be 180°.
But nights are cool.
And even during the day, it is cool inside the earth
where many animals live.

Some days, it rains.
All the world gets a little rain,
at least once in a while.
The desert may not get rain all year.
Or there may be only an inch or two.

Some rain doesn't even fall as far as the ground.
It starts from the clouds,
but it evaporates before it reaches the ground.

Other days, rain falls hard.

Drops come fast and big.

The ground cannot soak them all up.

The rain water runs off.

It runs as a river, and cuts a channel.

Then in an hour—or a day—the water drains
and the channel is dry.

Such channels are called dry washes.

The rain water forms lakes.

They soon evaporate and leave only sun-baked mud,
called dry lakes.

The rain water washes sand and rock from the mountains
and spills it in great sloping fans.

Rain brings life to the desert.
When there is enough rain, seeds sprout.
Plants grow.
Flowers open.
New seeds form.
When there is not enough rain, the seeds do not sprout.
They wait
. . . for a year or two,
or for ten years,
or more.

Palo verde and smoke trees live along dry washes. Even when the rivers are dry, water often is only a few feet under the sand.

Joshua trees live on hills and flats
away from the washes.
They keep their roots close to the surface of the ground.
The roots suck up rain as fast as it falls.

Saguaro cactus also has shallow roots.
Sometimes a saguaro sucks up too much water, too fast.
Its pleats swell and swell—until the plant bursts,
like a balloon with too much air.
But this is rare.

Most days, there is no rain.
Very few days have too much rain.

Cacti can do without rain for a long time if they have to.
They use the water already sucked up.
It is enough to let them grow
and flower,
while they wait for the next rain.
They can wait a year or more.

Cacti have thorns, but no leaves.
Leaves lose water to the air through tiny holes,
and cactus need to keep their water.
Their skins are green.
The skins do the work of leaves.
They make food for the plant.
Cacti skins are waxy. This helps keep the water inside.

Many desert plants have no leaves.
Their stems make the food.
Or they have waxy leaves which hold the moisture in,
or hairy leaves,
or tiny leaves that can't lose much water to the air.
Many plants grow leaves when there is rain,
and drop them when there is no rain.
Most desert bushes grow far apart.
A few ooze poison from their roots.
The poison kills new plants as soon as they sprout.
There isn't enough water for them all.

Animals must have water, too.
They cannot soak it up as plants do.
Sometimes they cannot drink,
because there are no pools of water.

Tarantula spiders . . .

and centipedes and others
get water from the juices of insects that they eat.

Some lizards, such as the horned toad
(which is really a lizard, not a toad),
also cat insccts.

Other lizards get their moisture
by eating plant leaves and flowers.

Kangaroo rats eat only seeds.
No moist leaves.
No juicy insects.
They never drink water.
Kangaroo rats live their whole lives
on the tiny bit of water that forms as they digest seeds.
They don't sweat or pant,
and they pass very little urine.
They sleep in cool holes in the ground all through the day.
At night, when the desert is cool, they come out
and hop about on their long hind legs, looking for seeds.

Kitfoxes come out at night too.
They come to hunt for kangaroo rats
and for mice and rabbits.
Kitfoxes get moisture as well as food
from the animals they eat.

Badgers also hunt small, nighttime animals
for moisture and food.

So do bobcats . . .

. . . and owls.

Each animal depends on other animals,
or on plants,
for its own life.

People think of the desert as hot and dry.
But for the animals and plants that live there
it simply is home.

RUTH and LOUIS KIRK lived in the desert at Death Valley, California, and along the Arizona-Mexico border—while Louis served as a ranger with the National Park Service. By jeep and on foot they explored the sand flats and canyons which newcomers find desolate, but which those who live in the desert see as beautiful.

From the desert, the Kirks moved to parks in the Dakotas and the Pacific Northwest. They live in Washington now, overlooking Puget Sound and the Olympic Mountains. Books, articles, filmstrips, and television programs have come from the team, portraying the natural history of the areas where they live and travel.